To GRANNY ZANNY

NEVER STOP LEARNING

LEARN

Grandpa's life lessons for one and all

originally written
4/12/2015

Kenn L. Custance

DEDICATION

Ulnumchxw siyaya

(All my relations)

4/12/2012

Kenn L. Custance

As he reminisced about his gifted life,
he spoke of tears, of joy, of strife.
"Many a day has come and gone,
And the things I've learned have made me strong.

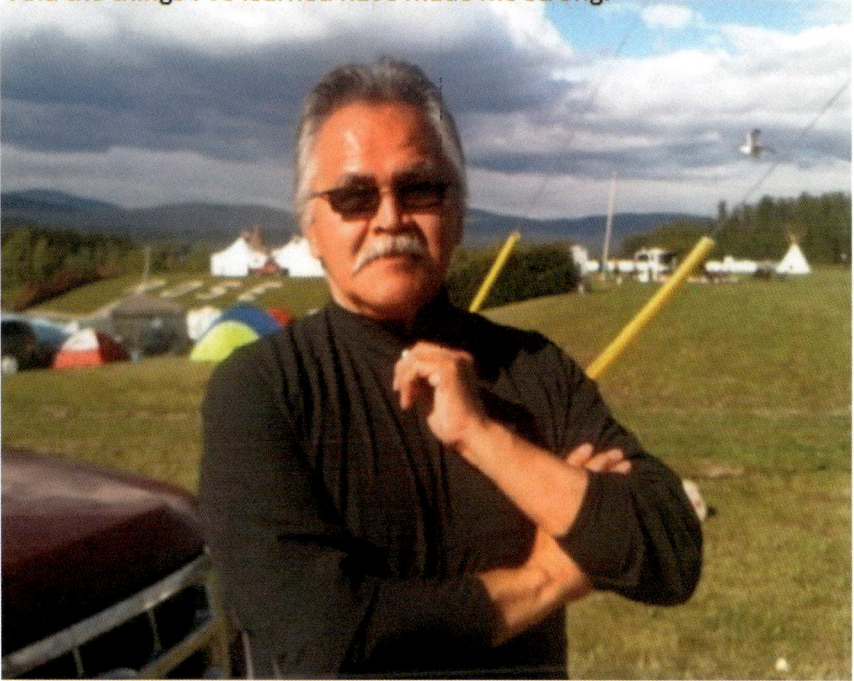

I'd like to share my point of view.
Take these lessons I've learned for you.
If you can learn from what I've done,
they will ease your life, Grandson.

Learn that it's okay to cry.
Learn that it's not okay to lie.

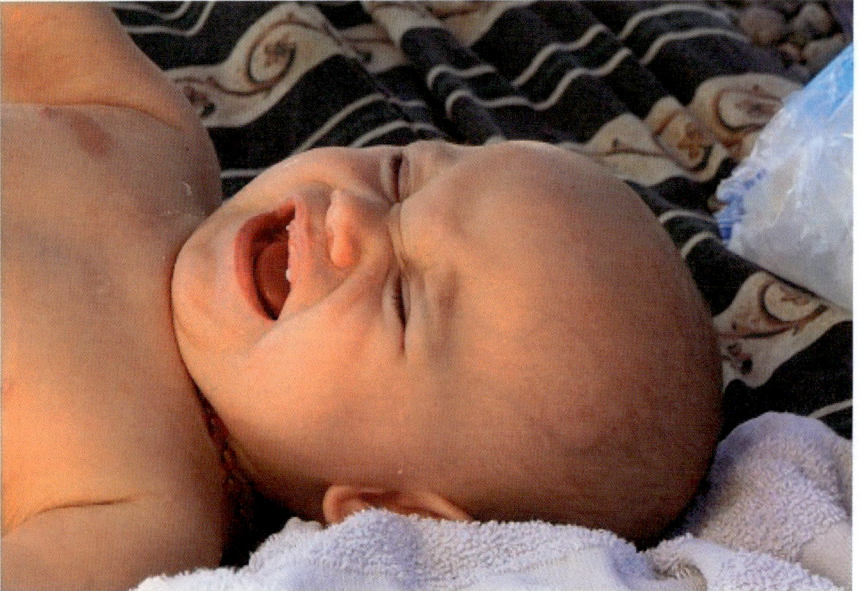

Learn that diapers aren't the only things smelling,
Learn it stinks when someone's yelling.

Learn that girls don't have germs.

Learn to hug on your own terms.

Learn in all people there is good and bad.

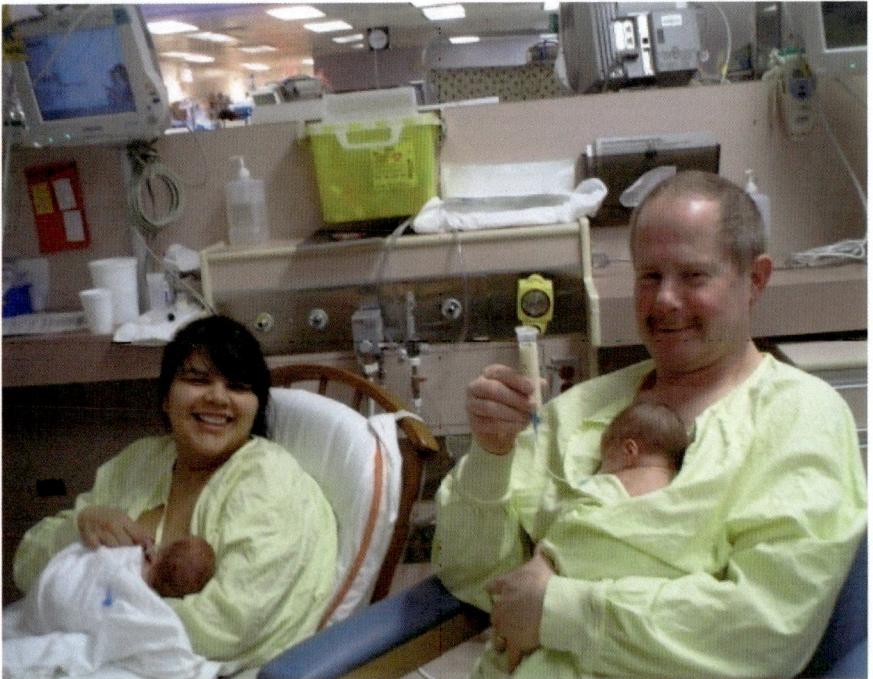

Learn that this includes Mom and Dad.

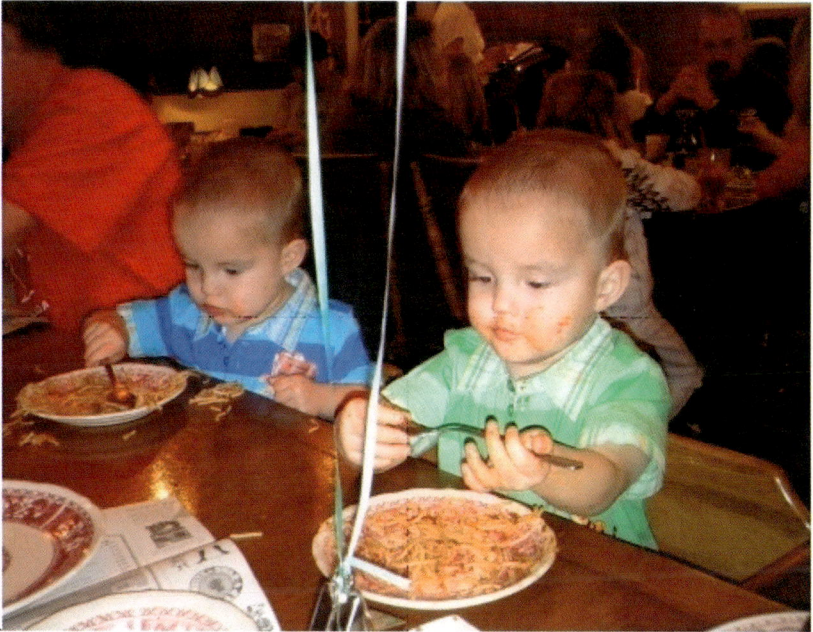

Learn to say 'thank you' and 'please'.
Learn to eat your carrots and peas.
Learn to chew your food well.
Learn your inside voice, and how to YELL!

Learn to live by the 'Golden Rule',
whether or not it is taught in school.

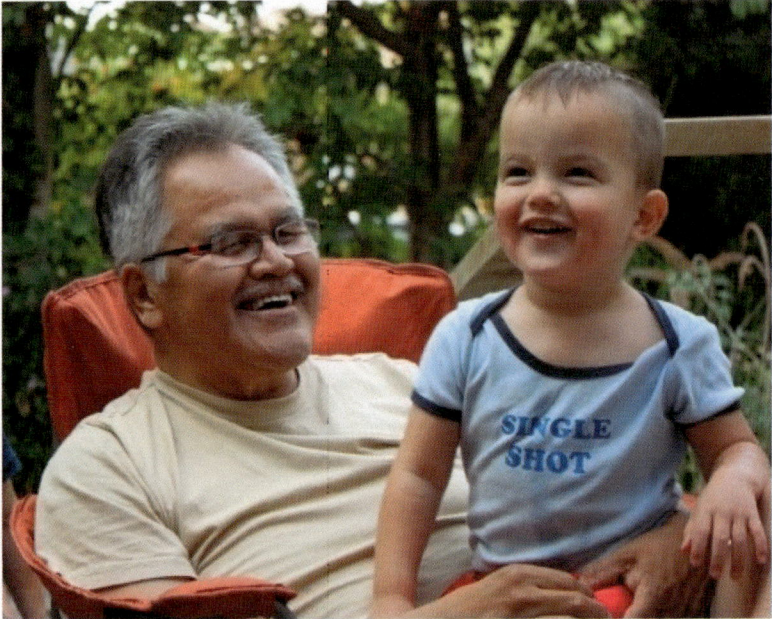

'Do unto others....', is how it goes.
It really is the best line ever, of prose.

Learn to enjoy every day.

Learn to laugh at life - to pray.

Learn what foods are good to eat.

Learn not to over-indulge in sweets.

Learn the value of brotherly love!
Learn not to hit, push, or shove!

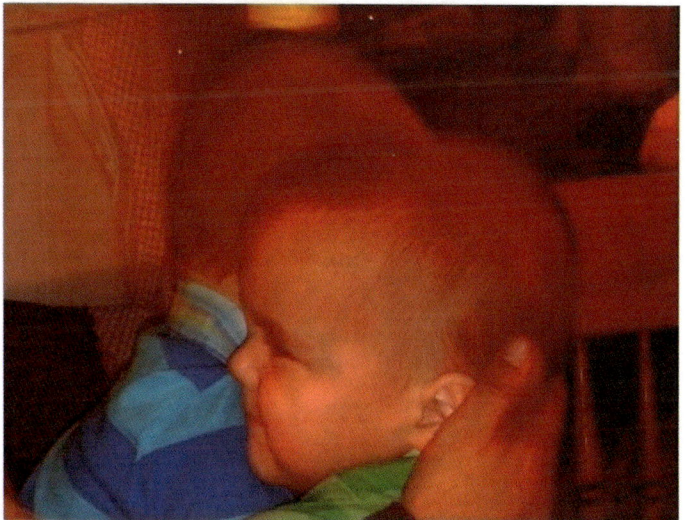

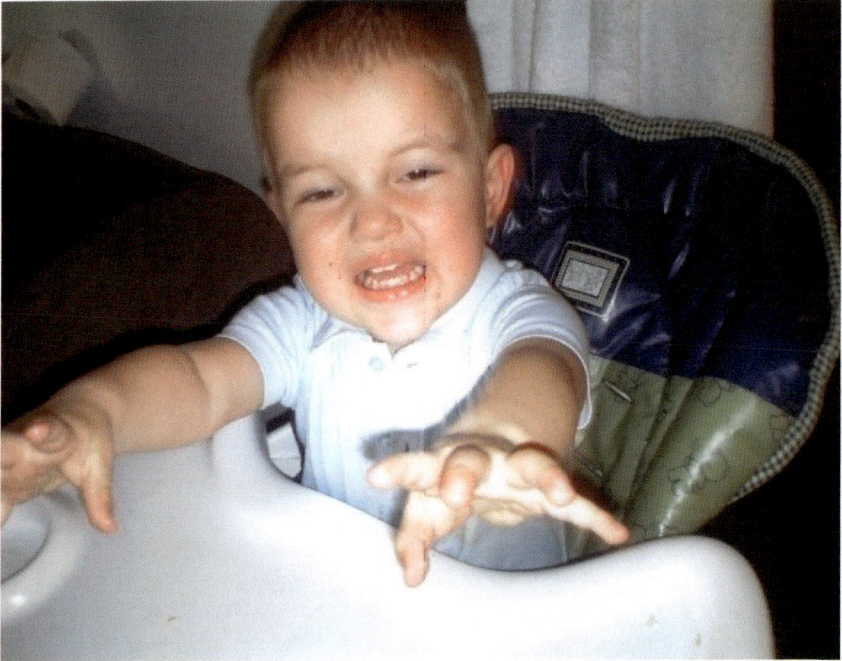

Learn you are important, that you have a voice!
Learn to accept the consequence of your choice!

Learn to walk,

to read,

And THRIVE!

Learn the joy to be ALIVE!

Learn how good it feels to give.
Learn how much it means to live.

Learn to walk at your own pace.

Learn life's a journey - not a RACE!

Learn to return what you find.

Learn it's not hard to be kind.

Learn not to want for possessions.
Learn to give sincere confessions.

Learn to pause, and take a breath.
Learn that part of life is death.

Learn two wrongs don't make a right.
Learn to only join a noble fight.

Learn that life is not always fair.

Learn to show how much you care.

Learn that happiness is fleeting.

Learn that it will be repeating!

Learn to appreciacte what you have!

Learn to appreciate WHO you have!

Learn to consider the source of what's said of you.
Learn - good or bad - do they count to you?

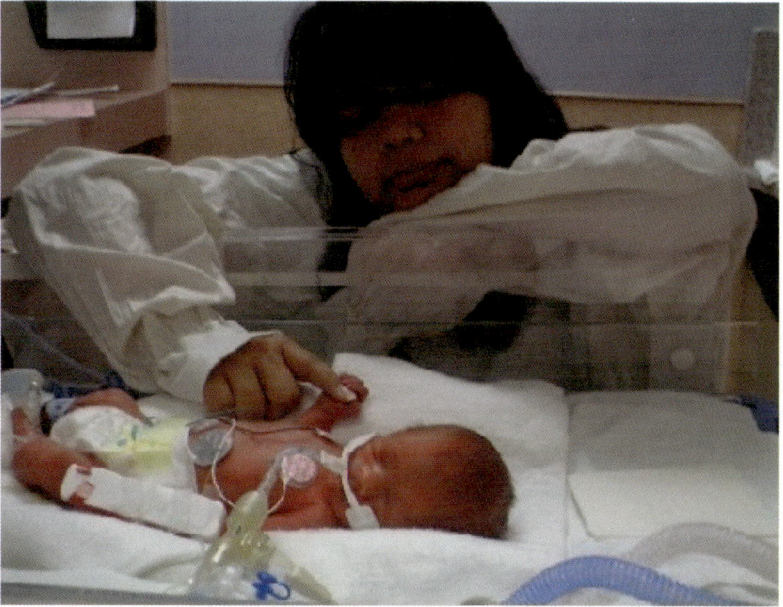

Learn that words can hurt, or heal.
Learn that you're in control of how you deal.

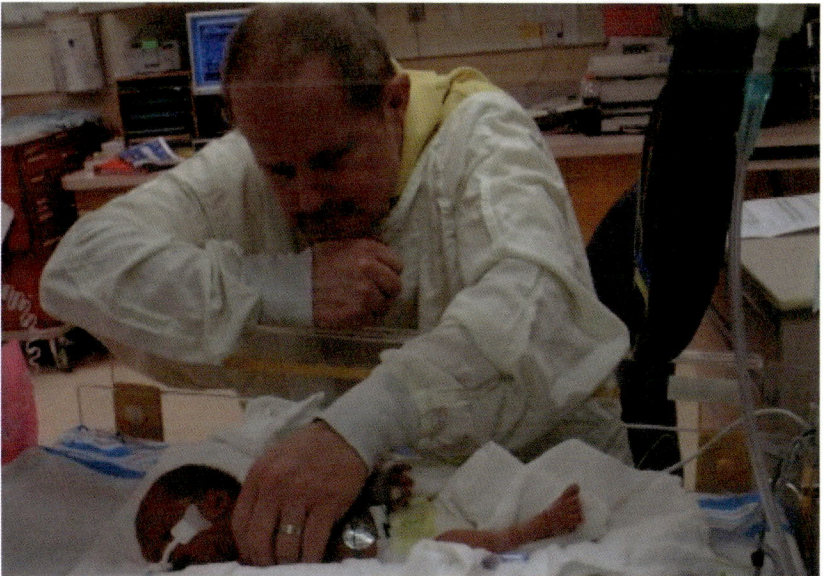

Learn that to earn respect is a two-way street.

Learn to walk down it with firmly-planted feet!

Learn to have a good work ethic.
Learn employers will respect it.

Learn to accept fair day's pay.
Learn to see things another's way.

Learn as you give, you receive.
Learn life goes on, and shortly grieve.

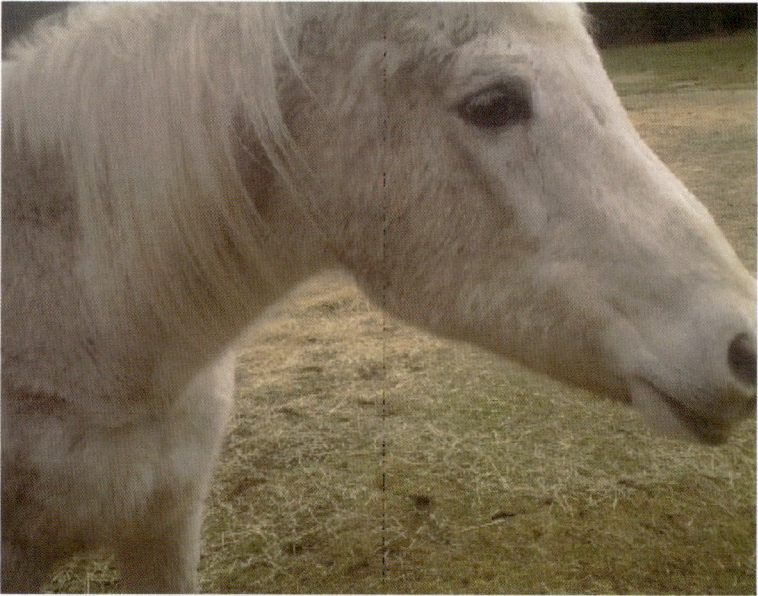

Learn not to join 'the fray'.
Learn to simply 'walk away'.

Learn high-five, in the middle , down low.
Learn to pat gently, when they're too slow.

Learn God's Word on your own.
Learn, by religion, you may be thrown.

Learn to cover your coughs and sneezes.
Learn not to lick metal when it freezes.

Learn to be wise with your money.
Learn it's good to laugh, and be funny.

Learn sometimes not to bend.
Learn sometimes it's okay to bend.

Learn your enemies, and learn your friends.
Learn to stay until the end!

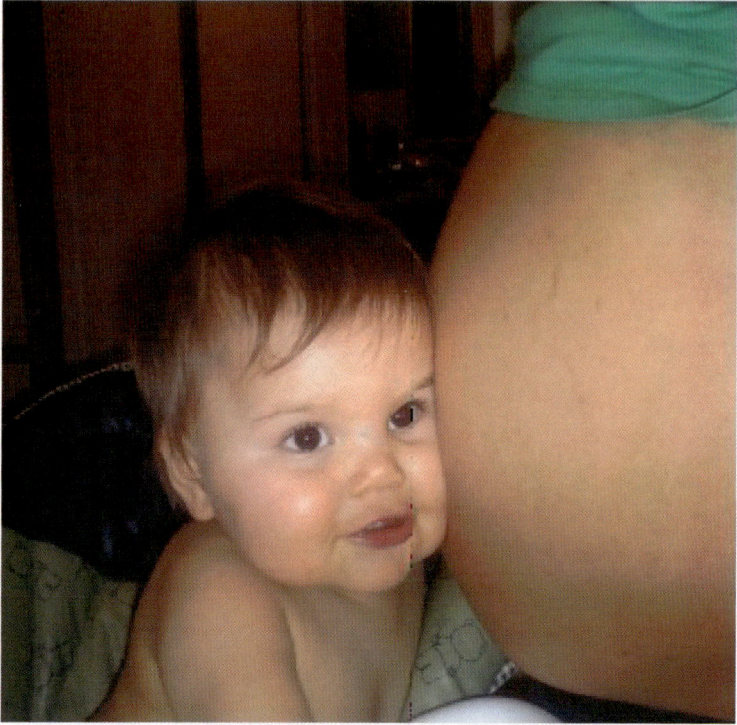

Learn to take that pregnant pause.

Learn how to tell a worthy cause.

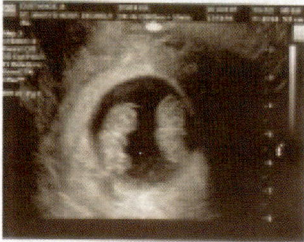 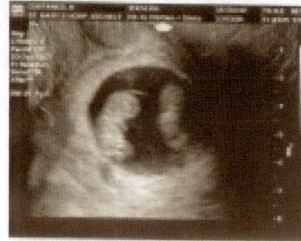

Learn to know when someone's messin'.

Learn not to lessen the lesson.

Learn that money won't make you happy.

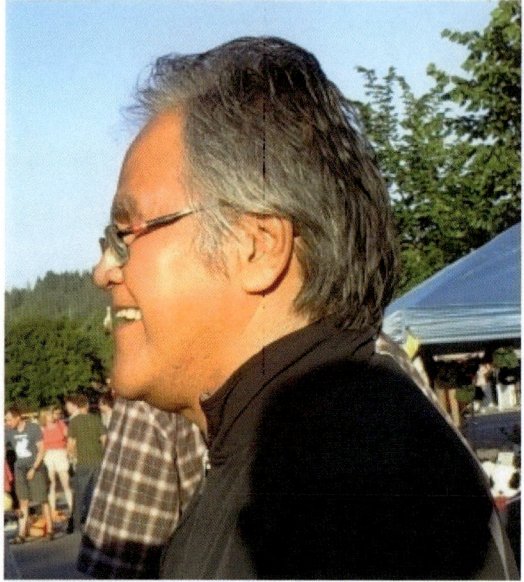

Learn to give all to your Pappy.

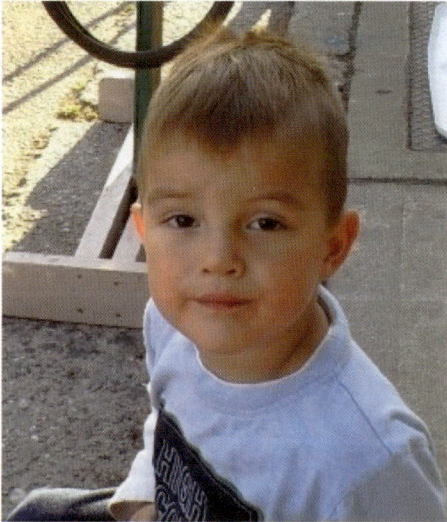

(just kidding.)

Learn that Gramma and Grampa love you,

and.......

Learn that Jesus Christ and His Dad, do too!"

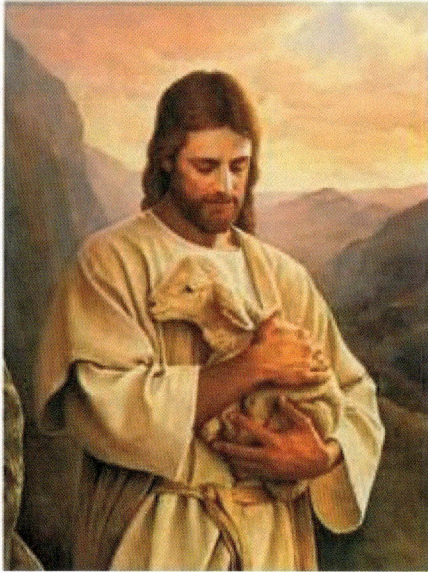

Made in the USA
Columbia, SC
05 June 2018